Jack —

X ma

Here is another source book
To further your legal understanding
By rigorous study & contemplation
you may, one day, be able to pass a bar
you will have arrived — "Discipline"

Love
Je

The
LAWYER
Joke Book

The LAWYER Joke Book

Perpetrated by Sid Behrman

Dorset Press
New York

This edition published by Dorset Press,
a division of Marboro Books Corp.,
by arrangement with James Charlton Associates.
1991 Dorset Press

Design and typography by Noble Publishers

Cover by Ziga Design

Some of the cartoons in this book have appeared in the following
publications and are reprinted by permission of the artists:

Cartoon on p. 65 © 1987 by Sidney Harris — *National Law Journal.*
Cartoons on pp. 30, 39, 54 are copyrighted by *The New Yorker.*

Printed in the United States of America

ISBN 0-88029-722-0

M 9 8 7 6 5 4 3

This book is dedicated to my lawyer who has steered me through wills, two divorce agreements, one prenupt, and several contracts. She was the inspiration and source for many of the jokes in this book. Cindy shall remain anonymous at her request.

An eager young attorney had just opened his first office. He'd decorated it with expensive, heavy oak furniture, a collection of costly art posters, and various other accoutrements to impress any potential client who walked through the door. He'd placed ads and sent out engraved announcements about his new business, and he was sitting back waiting for the phone to ring or his first client to appear.

Suddenly he heard the elevator doors closing and footsteps coming down the hall toward his office. He wanted to give the impression of a successful professional, so he grabbed the shiny new phone receiver and plunged into imaginary conversation.

"Yes, Mr. Torrence," he intoned as the stranger entered the office, "I'll attend to that business as soon as I've a free minute. I'm sure you're aware that Mr. Hollings had wanted me to handle his estate. I had to put him off, since I'm far too busy with other cases, but I'll manage to sandwich yours between the others

somehow. Yes, yes, certainly, it's my pleasure, sir. Goodbye."

Certain that he had properly impressed his prospective client, he hung up the receiver and turned to face the stranger, who was patiently waiting.

"Excuse me, sir," said the man, "I've come to connect your telephone."

———

An elementary-school teacher heard children wailing and crying and rushed to the playground to find out the cause of the disturbance.

"What's going on here?" she asked Marc, who sat on the jungle gym.

"Chuck took Laura's orange," explained the little witness. "Then she hit him on the head and called him a ninny and a jerk, and he kicked her in the stomach."

"Oh my, we'll all have to go the principal's office now," said the weary teacher. "And where is the orange?"

Marc smiled and produced the orange from his jacket pocket. "Oh, I have that. I'm Laura's lawyer."

At heaven's Pearly Gates, St. Peter warmly greeted a lawyer, then took his jacket and offered him a drink, some soft slippers, and a comfortable armchair. After the attorney was seated and sipping a martini, St. Peter handed him a remote-control for the television and a map showing his Jacuzzi, his tennis courts, and his private spa, all in his new 800-acre mansion.

The lawyer looked around in awe. "This is fabulous. Does everyone get this kind of treatment?"

"You're not just anyone, you know," St. Peter replied. "We don't often get a lawyer as distinguished and old as you."

"Old? Why, I'm only forty-eight," corrected the lawyer.

"Really? Well, isn't that funny. You've billed for so many hours we thought you were ninety!"

Frank Hoffman, a young attorney, was attending a funeral. A friend arrived a little late and seated himself, whispering, "At what stage of the service are they?"

Frank, pointing to the minister, whispered back, "He's just opening for the defense."

Frank Perdue's lawyer was working on an inspired scheme to sell more chicken. He called the Vatican and requested a private audience with the Pope. The request was refused, but the lawyer called again and again, and finally his request was granted. A few weeks later he was brought into a grand and stately room for an audience with His Eminence.

He knelt and kissed the Pope's ring and explained who he was and who he represented. Then he said, "Your Holiness, I have a proposition to make that I think could be of huge benefit to both of us. I'd like you to change the words of the Lord's Prayer from 'Give us this

day our daily bread' to 'Give us this day our daily chicken.' It will help my client sell more chickens, and we are prepared to pay the Church $1 million for this."

The Pope shook his head firmly and said, "No, young man, I am afraid that it is out of the question. The words to that holy prayer have remained unchanged for 2,000 years."

But the lawyer persisted. "Well, Your Holiness, would you do it for $5 million?"

"No, no," replied the Pope, "absolutely not. The Church holds tradition sacred and does not make changes casually."

The lawyer stood up. "All right, one hundred million dollars! Would you do it for one hundred million? Think of what you could do with that money!"

The Pope reflected silently upon the starving people around the world, the far-flung missions, and the myriad of other financial burdens on the Church. He looked over at the papal attorney before he nodded his assent. "Please tell Mr. Perdue that we have an agreement."

The next day, the Pope called a meeting of the College of Cardinals.

"Dearest colleagues," the Pope began, "I have for you some good news and some bad news. The good news is that we are receiving one hundred million from Mr. Frank Perdue to

change the words of the Lord's Prayer from 'Give us this day our daily bread' to 'Give us this day our daily chicken.'

"The bad news, friends, is that we're losing the Wonder Bread account."

———————

Corrupt businessman's telegram:
    RESULTS OF MY CASE?

Attorney's response:
    JUSTICE HAS TRIUMPHED!

Businessman's telegram:
    APPEAL IMMEDIATELY.

———————

Alimony is like buying oats for a dead horse.
    —Arthur "Bugs" Baer

Q. What do you call 500 lawyers at the bottom of the ocean?

A. A good start.

Fonseca, an unscrupulous lawyer for a man arrested for murder, bribed a man on the jury to hold out for a verdict of manslaughter.

The jury was out for a very long time, and finally they returned with a verdict of manslaughter. Fonseca rushed up to the juror.

"Here's your money," he said. "I'm much obliged to you, my friend. Did you have a very hard time?"

"Sure did," replied the man, "an awfully hard time. The other eleven wanted to acquit."

Mr. Giroux, a country lawyer, had led an exemplary life, representing clients honestly and professionally, never gouging or padding his fees, and donating his services to the indigent. When he died he was whisked straight to the Pearly Gates where St. Peter was waiting for him.

"Come right this way, Mr. Giroux," St. Peter gestured. "We've been awaiting your arrival, and your room is ready for you. Let me show you the sights as we walk."

The two set out, with St. Peter pointing out the magnificent scenery, the rolling hills, the waterfalls, the eighteen-hole championship golf courses, and the blossoming, exotic forests. It was breathtaking.

Soon they arrived at a modern apartment building that stretched hundreds of stories above the surrounding countryside. The two stepped into a glass elevator, and it rose automatically. Higher and higher it went, until it stopped and the doors opened, showing a luxurious apartment, decorated lavishly, with no expense spared. Awestruck, the lawyer started to step off.

"No, this isn't your apartment," St. Peter said.

"This belongs to Pope Matthew IV. Step back in."

He did, and the elevator rose another few floors until it reached the penthouse. There, the doors opened on an even more spectacular apartment that overlooked the vista on all four sides and contained a monorail just to shuttle the occupant around the many wings of the place. The lawyer was bewildered.

"There must be some mistake, St. Peter. This is even more beautiful than the apartment we just saw. And he was a Pope."

"Oh, it's no mistake," reassured St. Peter. "We get plenty of Popes up here, but you're our first lawyer."

―――――――

Martin and James had been partners in a firm for many years, and they shared and shared alike in nearly everything, including the affections of their young and hot-blooded secretary. One morning Martin came into James's office, obviously agitated.

"James," he moaned, "Sherry is pregnant! We're going to be a father!"

James, remaining calm, sat Martin down and pointed out that a great many worse things could have happened to them: losing the big Rosenbaum estate case, for instance. They agreed that the only thing to do was share the responsibility, as they had shared everything before.

Sherry would receive top-notch medical care, and after the baby was born, he or she would want for nothing. The child would have fine clothes, trips, the best private schools; they would set up a trust fund to guarantee their offspring's college education. The lucky child would have two fathers instead of one.

Soon enough, the big day arrived. Martin and James paced in the waiting room in a nervous frenzy. But James could not stand the tension any longer and said, "I'm going out in the parking lot and sit in the car; as soon as something happens, come and tell me."

Martin agreed, and in less than an hour he was out in the parking lot, wearing a grave expression.

"What happened? What is it?" shouted Martin.

"We had twins," James said sadly, "and mine died."

A lawyer was explaining the concept of ethics to his teenage son.

"Suppose a client came into your office for some legal advice about a contract," the father posited. "You discuss the matter and then bill him $100 for the advice. The client pulls out his wallet and hands you a crisp $100 bill, and then leaves.

"As you are putting the new bill in your wallet you see that he has given you not one $100 bill, but two $100 bills. Now comes the ethical question: Do you split the money with your partner?"

Mr. Milkums was briefing his witness, Ms. Harrison, before calling her to testify.

"You must swear to tell the absolute truth," the lawyer instructed. "Do you understand?"

"Yes, I'm to swear to tell the truth."

"Have you any idea what will happen if you

don't tell the truth?"

Harrison looked up.

"I expect our side will win."

———————

The devil went to the office of Ed Brown, a lawyer, with a proposition. Folding his tail under him, he sat down in the office and leaned forward.

"I'd like you to sell me your soul," he said wickedly.

The lawyer drummed his fingers on the desk.

"And what are you prepared to offer?"

"In exchange for your soul, I'll give you all the money you could ever want, plus fame, power, and respect."

The lawyer pondered the devil's words for several minutes.

"Hmmmmmmmm," he muttered. "There must be a catch."

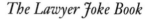

Professor Charlton said to Cecilia, one of his law students, "Now, if you were to give some- one an orange, what would you say to him?"

The student replied, "Here. I'm giving you this orange."

"No! No! No! Think like a lawyer, Cecilia!" shouted Professor Charlton.

"Okay. I'd say, 'I hereby give and convey to you all and singular, my estate and interests, rights, title, claim and advantages of and in, said orange, together with all its rind, juice, pulp, and pits, and all rights and advantages with full power to bite, cut, freeze, and otherwise eat, the same, or give the same away with and without the rind, skin, juice, pulp, or pits, anything herein before or hereinafter or in any other deed, or deeds, instruments of whatever nature or kind whatsoever to the contrary in anywise notwithstanding. . .'"

"Heaven knows, you couldn't ask for much more in a court-appointed lawyer."

21

A verbal contract isn't worth the paper it's written on.
  —Samuel Goldwyn

A passenger liner making its way from Miami to one of the Caribbean islands was caught in the middle of a fierce hurricane just a mile outside a safe harbor. The ship was violently tossed about by giant waves.

Suddenly, it foundered on a reef and a gaping hole was torn in the side of the ship. Water began to pour in. Quickly, the decision was made to abandon ship. As the last remaining lifeboat was being splintered by the reef, the first mate looked down and saw dozens of sharks circling the sinking ship. Quickly backing off, he huddled in fear with the rest of the passengers.

The ship's captain, a minister, and a lawyer gathered on deck to decide what to do. The captain looked down and declared, "I'll swim for help. I am the captain and have spent my

whole life at sea, and I'm familiar with the ocean and the currents." With that, he jumped in.

He was hardly wet when a giant white shark loomed up and swallowed him in one bite.

The minister then stepped forward. He looked up to heaven. "I am a man of God, and I will be protected." He dived in, only to be quickly eaten by another voracious shark.

The lawyer was next. Taking a deep breath, he plunged into the water. The school of sharks parted, and there was nothing but clear water ahead. The lawyer swam until finally he pulled himself up on shore.

He was immediately surrounded by rescuers. "It's a miracle!" one declared.

"Miracle, hell," the lawyer gasped. "It was professional courtesy."

—————

Q. How can you tell if it's a skunk or a lawyer that's been run over on the road?

A. There are skid marks around the skunk.

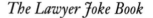

The young lawyer walked into the office of the senior partner. The older man could tell the lawyer was distressed and asked him to sit down.

"Jack, you seem upset. What's the matter?"

The young man rubbed his hands together. "It's this junk bond case we've been working on for months, Harry. The client, Clump, goes before the judge tomorrow, and I don't know what to do."

"Well, what are the options?"

Jack leaned forward. "The other lawyer on the case wants Clump to dress in a $3,000 suit, wear his Sulka tie and his Turnbull and Asner shirt, and show up at the courthouse in his chauffeured Cadillac. The lawyer thinks the judge will be intimidated by his importance and give him a light sentence."

Jack stood up and began pacing the office.

"I, on the other hand, think he should go down to a secondhand clothing store and buy an old sport coat, pick up a frayed shirt and a stained tie, not shave or bathe, and take a bus to the courthouse. I think the judge will be sympathetic to Clump's plight and give him a light sentence."

He shook his head. "So you can see the problem. What advice would you give Clump?"

The senior lawyer leaned back and thought a moment. Lighting his pipe, he started.

"You know Atkinson, that blonde paralegal? Well, she is getting married next week and came to me for some fatherly advice regarding her wedding night. Her sister had advised her to get her nails painted scarlet red, wear a short black peignoir with a plunging neckline, wear makeup, and dab heavy perfume behind her ears and knees. And she should make sure the lights were low and that there was romantic music playing softly on the radio. That was the way to meet her new husband.

"On the other hand, her mother had instructed her to buy a plain white-cotton nightgown with long sleeves and a tight neck, wear no makeup or perfume, and go to bed with all the lights off. So the poor girl had this conflicting advice and didn't know what to do."

The young lawyer was perplexed. "But what does this have to do with my client's case?"

The senior lawyer leaned forward.

"I'll give your client the same advice I gave her. It doesn't matter what you wear; either way you're gonna get screwed."

———

Alimony: The ransom that the happy pay to the devil.
—H. L. Mencken

———

The young attorney finished his summation: "And if it please the court, if I am wrong in this, I have another argument that is equally conclusive."

———

"That's a nasty-looking bunch of customers you've got to dispose of this morning, Your Honor," remarked the new court stenographer.

The veteran judge barely glanced up from the various documents he was reading. "You're looking at the wrong bunch. Those are the lawyers."

To some lawyers, all facts are created equal.
  —Felix Frankfurter

———

"Sarah, you just gotta marry me," pleaded the young man. "I can't wait another year. Why, I know a real quick way to make a million bucks," he said, grasping his sweetheart's hand as they swung in the porch swing.

"Oh? What?"

"Become a corporate lawyer, and work part-time."

———

Two little girls were having a heated argument.

Said Mindy, "My dad's better. He's an important carpenter. He makes buildings."

Replied Carol, "Oh, yeah? Well, my dad's a lawyer. He makes loopholes."

A hard-bitten attorney and a prim Anglican minister were seated next to each other on an airplane. After the plane had taken off, a pretty young flight attendant came along and asked if she could get them something to drink.

"I'll have a double whiskey and water," said the attorney. The drink was placed before him.

"Will you have a drink as well?" the flight attendant asked the minister.

The minister glared at her and the alcoholic beverages on her cart.

"I'd rather savagely rape a brazen whore than let liquor touch these lips," he icily declared.

Pushing his drink away, the attorney said delightedly, "I didn't know there was a choice."

Mrs. Pelegrino needed a lawyer and began flipping through the Yellow Pages. Finally she

came across Schwartz, Schwartz, Schwartz, and Schwartz. She dialed the number and said, "Good morning, is Mr. Schwartz there?"

A man replied, "No, ma'am, he's out playing golf."

"Well, then, I'll speak to Mr. Schwartz."

"Sorry, ma'am, he's not with the firm anymore; he's retired."

"Very well, let me speak to Mr. Schwartz, please."

"He's away in Detroit, ma'am, won't be back for a month."

"Ah, I see. May I speak to Mr. Schwartz, in that case?"

"Speaking."

———

Two henpecked husbands were downing a few beers and elaborating on the miseries of married life.

Frank looked over at his friend and sighed, "My wife should have been a lawyer. Every time we have an argument, she insists on appealing the decision to the higher court."

Paul looked at him. "You don't mean divorce court?"

Frank wearily shook his head. "No. Her mother."

EXTREME
CAUTION

LAWYERS
CROSSING

Stacey and Sabrina were wealthy, beautiful, successful Washington law partners. But Stacey suddenly fell ill with a mysterious disease, and her perplexed doctors could do nothing but declare she would die within a week. Her family were beside themselves with anguish; they called in experts from around the world, but the diagnoses were all the same, and Stacey resigned herself to her fate.

After taking care of professional and personal matters, she called her partner to her side and whispered, "Sabrina, I've been feeling horrible about this for two years now, and I guess there's really no reason to keep it from you any longer. Remember when we lost that big Johnson case? Well, Johnson's attorney paid me $400,000 not to call a key witness. We would have won the case, Sabrina. But I wanted the money. I took it, and I lost the case."

Her partner patted her hand.

"Don't worry about it, sweetie. Would you like some more cranberry juice? Can I get you another pillow?"

Stacey went on.

"And remember old Mrs. Epper? The one whose business we were supposedly going to

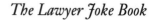
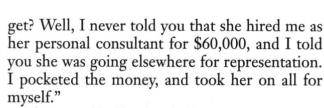

get? Well, I never told you that she hired me as her personal consultant for $60,000, and I told you she was going elsewhere for representation. I pocketed the money, and took her on all for myself."

Sabrina nodded her head. "Don't worry about it, it's fine, dear. Let me get you a cool washcloth."

"Sabrina, you are so good to me! I don't deserve this! I wish you'd get angry, or at least make me feel a little guilty!"

"Relax. Don't worry about it, dear, every-thing's fine now: I poisoned you."

Roy Cahn, one of the meanest and most suc-cessful lawyers in town, wrote his auto-biography last year. It began, "I borrowed $5,000 from my father so I could study law. My first case came when my father sued me for $5,000."

Fenwick, a shady businessman with interests all over the city, went to see Talbot, an attorney, but

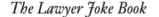
told her he wouldn't pay her unless she felt sure that there were grounds for legal action. He then gave her a lengthy account of the trouble.

After listening to him talk for more than two hours, the lawyer interrupted. "But Mr. Fenwick, your case is absolutely certain. The other fellow hasn't got a leg to stand on. You're absolutely in the right, and will win the case. So you owe me $200 for the advice."

"Nope—sorry," he said, and started to leave the office.

"What are you doing?" Talbot protested. You said you'd pay if I was certain your case was airtight, and it is—the other guy has no chance at all!"

Fenwick grinned. "I told you the other guy's side."

The day after his client was found guilty, lawyer Thompson rushed into court jubilantly waving a thick sheaf of papers.

"Your Honor, Your Honor," he cried. "I've just uncovered new evidence that requires reopening my client's case."

The judge stared at the lawyer. "New evidence?" the judge inquired. "What sort of evidence?"

"My client has an extra $10,000, and I only found out about it today!"

A well-known elderly judge had a case before him in which the plaintiff was being represented by a nervous young lawyer, Sara Ash. When she arose to begin her address, she tripped in approaching the bench and then dropped all of her papers. Finally, smoothing her hair, she began, "M-m-my unfortunate cl-cl-client . . ." and could not stammer out the next words. She tried again, and in a shaking voice warbled, "M-m-m-m-y un-un-un-unfortunate client . . ." and again she got stuck and could go no further. Clearing her throat, she took a deep breath and had another try: "My-my unfortunate cl-cl-cl-cl-cl-cl-client . . ." and again her voice failed. She looked around miserably.

"Come, come," interrupted the aged justice, "proceed with your statement. So far the court agrees with you."

A prisoner was in the dock on a serious charge of larceny in a small Midwestern county. The case having been presented to the court by the prosecuting attorney, the prisoner was ordered to stand up.

"Have you a lawyer?" asked the judge.

"Nossir," replied the fellow.

"Are you able to employ one?"

"Nossir, ah'm not."

"Do you want a lawyer to defend your case?" asked the kindly judge.

"Not partic'larly, Yer Honor."

"Well then," said the justice, clearly annoyed, "what do you propose to do about the case?"

"Far as ah'm concerned, sir," he said with a yawn, "ah'm willin' to drop the case."

Judge Bernuth peered down. "This is the fifth time you've been before me, young man."

"I know. When I like a fellow, I like to give him all of my business."

***

"Your Honor," said the jury foreman solemnly, "we find that the man who stole the $20,000 is not guilty."

***

Judges, as a class, display, in the matter of arranging alimony, that reckless generosity which is found only in men who are giving away someone else's cash.

—P. G. Wodehouse

At a very elite party in Beverly Hills, three professionals—a surgeon, an engineer, and an attorney—stood at the bar enjoying a martini. Each was successful, well known, and respected in his field. As the party proceeded and the drinks flowed, they became involved in an intense conversation. Philosophical issues arose, and soon they were debating what God's profession was when he created the planet Earth.

The surgeon spoke first. "Life only began after Eve was formed, and she was made when God removed one of Adam's ribs: clearly, a surgical procedure. Why, an engineer or an attorney couldn't have done it, and life would never have begun if God hadn't been a surgeon."

"Good point, my friend, good point," conceded the engineer. "But the thing is, God had to be able to create the actual world out of chaos. Only an engineer could build a marvelous, functioning planet out of chaos — "

"Yes, yes," interrupted the attorney, "but who created the chaos?"

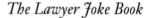
Two lawyers, disbarred for shady practices, met in the Lion's Head Pub.

"Hey, Hal! How's it going? What are you doing?"

"Well, Joe, I'm doing great! I'm in a related field, raking in twice as much dough as I did when I was a partner, and I have my own business."

"Really? What is it?"

"A witness business."

"What do you mean, a witness business?"

"No Matter What Happened, We Saw It, Incorporated!"

The pickpocket went to visit an old friend who had just been arrested.

"I had to hire a lawyer for you," he said, "and since I had no money, he asked me to leave my watch with him. I hope you appreciate this."

"Does he still have your watch?" asked his friend.

"He thinks he does."

"*And for God's sake stay as far away as you can from the legal system—unless, of course, you're a lawyer.*"

The judge solemnly regarded the case-hardened criminal snapping his gum and rolling his eyes in boredom. "Because of the gravity of this case," the judge said, "I am going to give you three lawyers."

"Never mind the three lawyers," replied the experienced defendant. "Just get me one good witness."

The case got huge publicity in the small mining town.

Mark was brought in on an assault charge. The state brought into court the weapons he used: a cat-o'-nine-tails, a rifle, a six-foot lead pole, a dagger, a pair of shears, and a chainsaw. Peter's counsel brought in the complainant's weapons: a scythe, a hoe, a mace, a shovel, a blowtorch, six empty cans of kerosene, a pitch-

fork, and a pair of tongs.

The twelve members of the jury filed slowly into the courtroom. The foreman rose, cleared his throat, and read the verdict: "We, the jury, would give $100 to have seen that fight."

―――――

The laws I love, the lawyers I suspect.
  —Charles Churchill

―――――

"You are to give the prisoner the best advice you possibly can," Judge Epperberger told the court-appointed lawyer as the court recessed.

Several hours later, the court reconvened but the prisoner was nowhere to be found. A search of the building and the grounds was made, and he still could not be located.

"Where in God's name is he?" Epperberger demanded of the attorney.

"Well, Your Honor," answered the lawyer

calmly, "I found out he was guilty as hell, so I told him to scram."

———————

The group of upstanding citizens was being given a tour of the local penitentiary.

A well-dressed matron said to a hardened old convict, "You poor man. Tell me, why are you here?"

"Well, lady," said the con, "my lawyer inherited $100,000 the day before he made his plea to the jury, and he couldn't cry."

———————

A woman was diagnosed as having a brain tumor and was told that she needed a transplant of a one-pound brain. Her doctor asked, "What kind of brain would you like?"

"I have a choice?" the woman said in astonishment.

"Yes," replied the doctor. "But there is a substantial difference in price. For example, a

one-pound brain of a surgeon costs $60,000, whereas a one-pound brain of a truck driver costs just $20,000."

The woman thought for a moment.

"Hmmmm. Can you get me a one-pound lawyer's brain? Ever since I was a little girl, I've dreamed of being a trial attorney."

"I can, but it'll cost you $250,000."

"But doctor, why so much?" the woman cried. "That's more than four times what the surgeon's brain costs!"

The doctor nodded. "Yes, but do you have any idea how many lawyers it takes to produce a pound of brain?"

Milton, fed up with his dog misbehaving, took his pet to the Jones Obedience School.

"Your dog can be trained to be anything you'd like him to be," said Jones.

This was more than Milton could believe. "Could you maybe give me a little demonstration?"

Jones then took a bunch of bones, threw them on the ground, and called, "Here, Fido." A dog rushed out, seized the bones, and five minutes

later had built a complicated bridge with them.

"That animal was trained for an engineer," announced the proud dog trainer, "and it only took six weeks."

"Incredible!" said the admiring Milton.

Jones dismantled the bones, threw them on the ground again, and called another dog. This animal quickly constructed an accurate skeleton.

"His owner is a doctor," explained Jones.

"Unbelievable," responded Milton excitedly.

Suddenly, a third dog rushed out, gobbled down all the bones, and then enthusiastically screwed the other two dogs.

"Great Scott!" exclaimed Milton. "Who owns that dog?"

"Oh, that one is being trained for a divorce lawyer."

———

A doctor and a lawyer were trying to have a discussion at a party. However, their conversation was constantly being interrupted by people asking the doctor for free medical advice about their operations, pains, and so on. After a half hour of this, the exasperated doctor turned to

the lawyer.

"What do you do to stop people from asking you for legal advice when you're out of the office?"

"Oh, I give it to them, and then I send them a bill," replied the lawyer casually.

The doctor was shocked, but it sounded practical and he decided he might give it a try.

The next day, still feeling slightly guilty, the doctor was undecided about the course of action the lawyer had advised. Then when he opened his mail, he found a bill from the lawyer.

———

For five years, a young attorney had been taking his vacations at a certain country inn. He'd always had an eye for the innkeeper's daughter, who had blossomed into a beautiful young woman. On his last visit a year ago he had managed to entice her into bed with him.

On vacation again, he stepped out of the taxi, and he carried his suitcase up the front stairs of the inn. Then he stopped short. There sat his lover with a baby on her lap!

"Jackie Sue, why didn't you write when you

learned you were pregnant?" he cried. "I would have rushed up here, we could have gotten married, and the baby would have my name!"

"I thought about it," she replied. "When my folks found out about my condition, we sat up all night talking about what to do. Finally, we decided it would be better to have a bastard in the family than a lawyer."

And whether you're an honest man,
Or whether you're a thief,
Depends on whose solicitor
Has given me my brief.
   —W.S. Gilbert

Smithfield said to his wife, "It is about time we found out what Matthew wants to be when he grows up. Watch this."

He put a $10 bill on the table and explained,

"That represents a banker."

Next to it he put a brand new Bible. "This represents a minister."

Beside that he placed a bottle of whiskey. "That represents a bum!"

The two of them then hid where they could watch the table without being seen. Pretty soon Matthew walked into the room, whistling, and noticed the three things on the table. He looked around to check that he was alone. Not seeing anyone, he picked up the money, held it to the light, then put it back down. He then thumbed through the Bible, and put that down. Then he quickly uncorked the bottle and smelled its contents. In one quick motion, he stuffed the money into his pocket, put the Bible under his arm, chugged down the contents of the bottle, and walked out of the room, still whistling.

The father turned to his wife and whispered, "How about that? He's going to be a lawyer!"

Roger was sick of big-city life in Chicago. Finally, he sold his apartment, quit his job, and moved to a tiny town in North Dakota. Trouble

followed him, though, and it was not many months later that he went to the general store and spoke to the grizzled old proprietor. "I need some legal advice, Henry," he said, "and I was wondering, is there a criminal lawyer here in town?"

"Why, ah reckon so," answered the cautious shopkeeper, "but ah don't know as we kin prove it on him."

———

Attorney Kellock got his client a suspended sentence: they hanged him.

———

The prosecuting attorney approached the witness.

"Do you happen to know any of the people you see in the jury box?"

The witness looked them over and thought carefully before replying. "Yes, I know more than half of them."

"Keep in mind the solemn oath you have made before this court," continued the attorney. "Can you swear that you know more than half of them?"

"Why, I most certainly can!" the witness fired back. "In fact, I'll swear I know more than all of them put together!"

Mrs. Hunter was called to serve for jury duty, but asked to be excused because she didn't believe in capital punishment and didn't want her personal thoughts to prevent the trial from running its proper course. But the public defender liked her thoughtfulness and quiet calm, and tried to convince her that she was appropriate to serve on the jury.

"Madam," he explained, "this is not a murder trial! It's a simple civil lawsuit. A wife is bringing this case against her husband because he gambled away the $12,000 he had promised to use to remodel the kitchen for her birthday."

"Well, okay," agreed Mrs. Hunter. "I'll serve. I guess I could be wrong about capital punishment after all."

Said the cynical and weary Mullane to his drinking buddy: "Y'know, I could always spot a lawyer when he's lyin'."

"Oh yeah? How's that?" asked his pal.

"His lips are movin'."

The chairman of a charity fund drive undertakes a big chore by calling on a wealthy lawyer and trying to get him to contribute money.

The chairman gets an appointment with the lawyer and goes to the office.

And the chairman says, "You know, you've never contributed to our charity. Our research shows you made over $400,000 last year, and we feel you should give something."

And the lawyer answers, "Did your research show that I have a mother with no means of support? Did it show that my sister's husband

was killed in a terrible accident, leaving her with four small children? Did it show that my brother was badly injured in the Vietnam War?"

"No, sir," replied the chairman meekly, ashamed.

"Well, if I don't give anything to them, why should I give anything to you?"

A farmer in East Bumblehoot caught a young woman gallivanting about his property in her birthday suit and had her hauled before the county magistrate.

"What's the charge?" inquired the elderly honorable.

"Bathing in the spring, Your Worship," answered the farmer.

The judge consulted an ancient dog-eared textbook and buried himself in its pages, muttering and stroking his beard. Then, closing the legal tome, he solemnly stated, "This here charge is dismissed, and the lady released. I find she has just as much right to bathe in the spring as she do in the fall."

The defendant appeared before a New England judge and, hoping for leniency, pleaded: "Your Honor, I'm down and out . . ." Whereupon the judge replied, "You're down, friend, but you're not out. Six months."

Michael needed some legal advice, and all of his friends warned him about lawyers—they were a mean and greedy bunch, they all agreed. However, he had no choice, so he looked in the phone book and found the name of Ben Blagdon. He made an appointment and was ushered in to see the lawyer. Remembering his friends' advice, he was on guard.

"First things first, Mr. Blagdon. What's your fee for a consultation like this?"

"Five hundred dollars for three questions."

Michael was taken aback. "Are you serious? Isn't that a bit steep for three measly questions?"

"It sure is. What's your third question?"

———

The illegal we do immediately. The unconstitutional takes a little longer.
—Henry Kissinger

———

The judge's gavel slammed down, bringing the trial to a conclusion. Lawyer Shields shook hands with his client, who had been found innocent, and then presented him with a bill.

The client looked at the figure and gulped.

"This says I have to pay $1,000 now, and $500 a month for the next five years! It sounds like I'm buying a Mercedes."

The lawyer beamed. "You are."

Magistrate: "Can't this case be settled out of court?"

Mueller: "Why, Your Honor, that's what we were trying to do when the police interfered."

Marcia, the lawyer's wife, was complaining.

"Just look at our house, Bart! It's disgraceful, and our neighbors are talking about us. The furniture is old, the carpets are worn, the house needs painting. It's a mess," she whined. "We need a complete redecoration."

"Honey, honey, don't worry, just be patient," Bart pleaded. "I just got a new divorce case today, and as soon as I break up their home, I can fix up ours."

The law professor leaned over his lectern and addressed the eager young faces. "The U.S. is the number one country in the world in terms of the quantity of lawyers; we have more than anyone else. But we are facing a crisis," he warned. "If we don't start producing more criminals, some of the lawyers will have to go on welfare!"

At a crowded cocktail party, Dr. Millstein and attorney Levy were arguing.

"I do ten operations a day," crowed the doctor. "I've got my techniques down perfectly. Every operation is successful. You, on the other hand, try cases and advise clients in a very imprecise fashion. What do you have to say for yourself?"

Levy looked at him and nodded his head. "You're right. In my field, my practice doesn't make me perfect. It just makes me rich."

Three young boys climbed over the fence into Farmer Bell's huge orchard, burgeoning with fresh new apples and pears. The boys gorged themselves, then threw more fruit around and tore the place up. When Farmer Bell happened upon them, they were in the midst of stripping his biggest apple tree of all its fruit. The angry farmer was certain he would suffer a huge loss and insisted on pressing charges.

The three boys were dealt with harshly by

their families. When the contrite threesome appeared in court with their angry parents behind them, the judge took pity on them. He asked them if they had learned from the experience.

Freddy spoke up first. "Your Honor, my dad's a doctor, and I know now that eating fruit that isn't fully ripe can make me real sick, and I'm never going to do it again."

Bobby then spoke. "Me neither, Your Honor. My dad's a professor, and he says I'll never get to college with a criminal record. I swear I'll never do it again, sir."

"I won't do it again, either," the third boy added. "But my daddy's a lawyer, and I'm gonna sue farmer Bell for damages. His damn fence tore my new jeans!"

If the laws could speak for themselves they would complain of the lawyers in the first place.
—Lord Halifax

A jury consists of twelve persons chosen to decide who has a better lawyer.
—Robert Frost

A potential client asked his lawyer what he would charge for taking on a particular case.

After considering the merits of the case, the lawyer answered that he would take it on for a contingency fee.

"What is a contingency fee?" asked the client.

The lawyer smiled. "A contingency fee means that if I don't win your suit, I don't get anything. If I do win your suit, you don't get anything."

A man was charged with stealing a horse, and after a long trial, the jury acquitted him. Later

in the day, the man came back to see the judge who had presided at the hearing.

"Judge," he said, "I want to get out a warrant to arrest that dirty lawyer of mine."

"What's the matter?" asked the surprised judge. "He won your acquittal, didn't he? What do you want to have your lawyer arrested for?"

"Well, Your Honor," replied the man, "I didn't have the money to pay his fee, and so he went and took the horse I stole!"

A lawyer had a dripping faucet in his office bathroom. He looked in the Yellow Pages and found the number for a nearby plumber.

The plumber arrived and easily took the entire faucet apart. Within five minutes, it was put back together, with the faulty washer replaced. Wiping his hands, the plumber said, "That will be $150."

"What?" gasped the astonished lawyer. "That's more money than I make in an hour!"

Nonplussed, the plumber looked at him. "I know. That's why I quit being a lawyer."

In divorce court, the lawyer and his client were standing in front of the judge, awaiting the decision.

The judge looked over at the weeping ex-wife, then looked down at the ex-husband, and declared, "The court shall grant this woman $500 a week in alimony."

The ex-husband looked up. "That's very nice of you, Your Honor. Why, I'll even kick in a few bucks myself."

One day a lawyer died and went to heaven.

When he arrived at the Pearly Gates, St. Peter asked him, "Who were you?"

The man told him, "I was a New York City divorce lawyer."

St. Peter studied the man suspiciously, and said, "We do have our standards here, you know. What exactly have you done to earn eternal happiness?"

The lawyer thought about it at great length

and searched his mind for one good deed. Finally, he recalled an incident. "As a matter of fact, the other day I saw a bum on the street, and I gave him a quarter," he said, beaming.

St. Peter, nodding grimly, looked over to his assistant Gabriel and asked, "Is that in the records?"

Gabriel nodded his head in assent. Peter then said, "Well, that's not very impressive, nor is it enough. I'm sorry," he said, and turned to close the gate.

"Wait, wait, there's more!" shouted the man. "The other night, I was walking home from the theater, and I tripped over a homeless boy. I stopped and gave him a quarter."

Peter again asked his assistant for confirmation, and again Gabriel checked the records and found it to be true. "Is there anything else?" Peter asked.

The lawyer thought hard and finally said, "No. Not that I can think of."

St. Peter contemplated him for a long moment, and then asked Gabriel, "Well, what do you think we should do?"

Gabriel glanced at the lawyer disgustedly and said, "I say we give him back his half a buck and tell him to go to hell."

One day the gate between heaven and hell fell off its hinges, as happened from millennium to millennium. St. Peter went to the scene and called down to the devil.

"Hey, devil, it's your turn to fix the gate. We did it the last time, a few million years ago."

The devil yelled back up, "Sorry, Peter, my boys are too busy to fix it now."

"All right, Lucifer," retorted St. Peter, "we'll have to sue you for breaking our agreement."

The Devil grinned. "Great idea, but where are you going to find a lawyer?"

Drucker was a coroner who vehemently despised those of the legal profession; he found them obnoxious, greedy, and cold. Thus it was with great reluctance that he testified at the trial of a man accused of murdering a lawyer. The defense attorney, after seeing him sworn in, approached him with a set of questions.

"Doctor, isn't it the case that you didn't per-

sonally know the victim, attorney Alvin Discus?"

"That's so," answered Drucker.

"And you did not yourself verify the identification of the victim as attorney Alvin Discus?"

"True," acknowledged the doctor.

"So isn't it actually true that, as far as you know, attorney Alvin Discus may still be among the living?" thundered the defense attorney.

"Oh yes, you're quite right," replied Drucker quietly. "His brain is in a jar at the morgue, but the rest of him may very well be out practicing law somewhere!"

The lawyer was hired to represent the son of a wealthy New York businessman in all of his court appearances, which tended to occur with alarming frequency.

The boy was always getting in trouble; however, his attorney was the very best in the state and much sought after, and he always managed to get the boy off. In fact, it injured the man's pride to have to represent the boy and clear him of all repercussions from his antics, but his

father was a needed and important client with many political connections.

One night, the attorney came to bail him out of jail after he'd been picked up for drunk driving. He was disgusted to have been woken up at three o'clock in the morning and said, "You know, young man, I've half a mind not to represent you this time, and let the law run its course with you; maybe that would teach you not to treat the law as if it were a joke."

"But sir, I swear to goodness, I only had one for the road!"

"Mmmmmm? And how many for the ditch?"

———

After the death of his wife, Mr. Binswanger bought a small dog. With nothing else to distract him, he trained the animal night and day. He taught the dog to sit and roll over, and to jump through a hoop.

But being the devout man that he was, he felt that all the tricks were worthless if the dog was not doing something that honored God in some way, and he decided that the animal needed to observe some religious rituals. He taught the

"There's a very good reason why I prefer you not to plead your own case in this court. You are depriving some worthy lawyer of the opportunity to turn a fast buck."

dog to wear a yarmulke and to rock slowly back and forth at the sound of praying.

When the dog had mastered the maneuver, he took him to temple. When the prayers began, the dog began to daven.

The man next to Binswanger nudged him and said, "That dog looks like he is praying!"

"Yes," said Binswanger. "Isn't it wonderful?"

"You know, Binswanger," said his neighbor, "that dog could make a fortune on TV."

"I know," said Binswanger, "and I have asked him to do it. But he wants to be a lawyer!"

———————

Ralph, a lawyer, was being nagged by his wife to tell their young teenage son about the birds and the bees.

"You want him to grow up knowing nothing about sex? You want him to find out about it on the street, or from his friends?"

She went on, "I don't care if it makes you uncomfortable. You're a successful, confident lawyer, and you can tell him. You've got to have a talk with him, Ralph."

Reluctantly, the father knocked on his son's bedroom door and went in. Pacing back and forth, he started, "Son, we need to have a talk."

"Sure, Dad, what about?"

"About the alleged facts of life."

Q. What's a lawyer?

A. Someone who reads a 10,000-word document and calls it a brief.

Q. What's a judge?

A. Someone who's stopped practicing law.

Q. Why does New Mexico have so many vultures and Washington have so many lawyers?

A. New Mexico had first choice.

Did you hear about the well-known shyster lawyer?

He came down with pneumonia . . . from settling all of his cases out of court.

Legal secretary to amorous boyfriend: "Stop and/or I'll slap your face."

Some people think about sex all the time, some people think of sex some of the time, and some people never think about sex: they become lawyers.

—Woody Allen

Retired professor Moriarty was brought before the country judge on charges.

The judge said sternly, "This is not the first time you have been brought before this court on charges of being drunk and disorderly. Have you any reason why a stiff sentence should not be pronounced?"

The old drunk stood up and looked at the judge. "Man's inhumanity to man makes countless thousands mourn."

Then he turned and faced the courtroom. "I'm not as debased as Poe, as ungrateful as Keats, as intemperate as Burns, as timid as Tennyson, as vulgar as Shakespeare, as —"

The judge interrupted, "Shut up! That'll be ninety days." And he slammed down the gavel. Then he said to the bailiff, "Take down that list of names and round them up, they're as bad as he is!"

"Are these your witnesses?" asked the prosecuting attorney.

"They are," replied the defense counsel.

"Then you win. I've had those witnesses twice myself."

Overheard in the supermarket checkout line: "Her lawyer is honest, but not enough to hurt her case."

———

"Smith, you're sentenced to twenty days on bread and water; how d'ya like that?"

"Toasted?"

———

Harry, a down-and-out attorney, was sitting at the end of the bar nursing a whiskey when a former colleague sat down.

"How's business, Harry?" asked the man.

Harry shook his head. "I just got eviction papers," he said mournfully. "I wrote them up myself. I wouldn't have done it if I didn't need the money."

———

Harold explained to Jennifer why he was so determined to enter law school:

"I don't like money, but it settles my nerves."

71

It is hard to believe that a man is telling the truth when you know that you would lie if you were in his place.
—H. L. Mencken

Three heart-attack victims stood before St. Peter, hoping to be admitted to heaven.

"And how did you suffer your heart attack, ma'am?" he asked the shapely woman before him.

"My husband caught me making love with the milkman," she sheepishly admitted.

"I'm sorry, my dear, but I'll have to send you to hell for that. Please enter the elevator behind you."

He turned to the next arrival. "And you, sir? What were the circumstances of your death?"

"I had a heart attack when the IRS called me. It seems they had caught up with me after I had cheated on my income tax for thirty years!"

St. Peter shook his head. "I'm terribly sorry to

hear that, sir. Please step into the elevator behind you. You'll have go to hell."

He turned to the last applicant. "And how about you, sir? How did your heart attack happen?"

The man looked down. "It happened when I opened the mail this morning and found my lawyer's bill."

"Ah," said St. Peter, "please go through the gates."

———

Marshall's suit against Moregood was interrupted by the Thanksgiving holiday. Marshall, a poultry farmer, asked his attorney if it wouldn't be a good idea to send the judge a nice, plump young turkey.

"Good God, no!" shouted his counselor. "That would mean losing the case for certain. The judge would think you were trying to influence him."

Marshall met with his attorney the day before court was to convene again and mentioned, "Well, I sent that turkey."

"You fool! You're insane! Now you've no

chance of winning the suit!"

"Don't you go screaming," admonished Marshall. "I sent that turkey all right, but I put Moregood's name on it."

Organized crime is a blight on our nation. While many young Americans are lured into a career of crime by its promise of an easy life, most criminals must work long hours, frequently in buildings without air-conditioning.
—Woody Allen

Judge Rottblot was a hardened old man; he'd seen it all and heard more unbelievable stories than he could remember. Yet for some reason, the prostitute's hardships moved him. She was sixty years old, and she had been beaten and abused and left to starve. She did not have any marketable skills other than her pathetic body,

and she was just mentally deficient enough to prevent her from learning a trade. While he was sitting in a coffee shop and pondering the case, a colleague whom he respected entered and sat at the counter.

"Excuse me, Larry," said the judge. "What would you give a sixty-year-old hooker headed for nothing but hell?"

His friend replied, "Ten bucks, maximum."

In a desperate act, Felix, a bank teller, quietly let himself into the vault and filled his briefcase with $100 bills, then fled home. He quickly came to his senses and realized the enormity of his action.

He phoned his attorney and said, "I've stolen $50,000 from the bank I work for! I don't know what came over me! What should I do?"

"Steal $50,000 more and bring it to me," the attorney directed calmly.

Felix was astounded, but he did it, and after he brought her the cash, she wrote the following letter, which served to get the man off:

"Gentlemen: Your teller, Felix Fingers, took

$100,000 from your bank. The hard-pressed family, despite their most valiant efforts, was unable to raise more than $50,000, which they offer to return if you will not prosecute . . ."

Heifitz was fuming. "I'm gonna sue that lowlife for label!" he screeched.

"Libel. You mean libel," corrected his patient attorney.

"No, I mean label!" shouted Heifitz. "I make good suits. He makes crappy suits and uses my label!"

A lean award is better than a fat judgment.
—Benjamin Franklin

Brendan was arrested for speeding, reckless driving, driving without headlights, and violating traffic signals. He demanded a trial by jury.

"But you can't win that in court," advised his friend Mike.

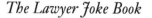

"I know," replied Brendan, "I did it on purpose. My nephew just got out of law school and this is going to be his first case. I want him to lose, then maybe he'll get discouraged and get an honest job."

Frankie had always been compulsively neurotic. One day, he locked on to a question and couldn't function until he knew the answer.

"What is one plus one?"

He shook and he shuddered. He was filled with an uncontrollable need to find the answer. He pulled out a phone book, flipped it open, and found the address of a psychologist. He hurried to the office and poured out his urgent question to the doctor.

The doctor sat back in his chair, scratched his beard, and then informed Frankie that with three or four years of triweekly counseling sessions, they would certainly be able to uncover the answer.

Frankie stumbled out of the office. He then located an engineer. Frankie emptied his pockets to the man, pleading and crying hysterically

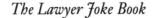
that he be given an answer.

The engineer began making notes, scribbling on little scraps of paper, and feeding information into his computer. Finally, he told Frankie that the nearest physical approximation, in the whole-number system, was 1.987544678789786, which could be rounded to 2, if necessary, in the third-dimensional plane.

Frankie was distraught and fled.

A few blocks away he saw a sign advertising a lawyer. He went into the building and took an elevator up. He rushed into the quiet, elegant office and moaned his question out to the lawyer.

The lawyer came around to the front of the desk and took each of Frankie's hands, looking calmly into his eyes. He said, "What would you like it to be?"

"It is my understanding that you called on the plaintiff," stated Counselor Lutkin.

"I did," replied the witness.

"What did he say?"

The prosecutor leapt to his feet and slammed down his book, vehemently objecting to the question. He denounced the question as irrelevant, misleading, and tending to incriminate an entirely innocent party. He accused Lutkin of using illegal tactics, and of being a wholly immoral person, guilty of malicious practices by daring to try to introduce such testimony. He continued, questioning the legitimacy of Lutkin's birth, the decency of his mother, and the marital conduct of his wife.

Lutkin, boiling with rage, jumped for the prosecutor's throat, and court attendants were forced to subdue the two antagonists, but not before they'd bloodied each other's noses and blackened each other's eyes.

The judge, after restoring order, ruled that Lutkin would repeat the question and directed the witness to answer.

The court fell into a deep silence, waiting to hear the crucial testimony.

Wiping blood from his upper lip, Lutkin said, "I repeat, then: What did he say?"

The witness answered, "He didn't say anything. He wasn't home."

Q. How many lawyers does it take to change a lightbulb?

A. How many can you afford?

A professor of second-year law students suspected that his pupils were not paying attention to the lecture and decided to test them.

"Therefore," he intoned, "in reference to the penal section regarding hoffenwerg, it is necessary to take steps involving raganny of the twoozer, innebblety of the fourth gipp, and a thorough examination of all relevant croatary oxance."

Calls a student from the back of the room: "Fine, but what the hell is the fourth gipp?"

Sign in the office of Tony Soricillo, estate attorney: "Where there's a will, there's a delay."

A lawyer died and was being given a tour through hell by an associate devil.

"Step lively, sir," he directed. "Please observe everything you see carefully as we go, because after you have seen all of hell, you will have to choose the room in which you want to spend eternity."

The first room was pitch-black, and blood-curdling screams issued from inside. Then came the hideous sound of cracking bones and snapping tendons. The man shuddered and cried, "Not this room!"

The second room they came to was well lit, and the man peered inside. Strapped to a table was an emaciated man licking his lips and begging for water. "Certainly not this room," said the lawyer, quivering.

The next room was pleasantly lit, and inside

they saw people standing knee-deep in manure, drinking cups of coffee and tea.

"Well, compared to the others, this room doesn't seem too unbearable. I guess I'll take this one."

With that, the demon shoved him into the room and locked the door behind him. The lawyer stood still for a moment, getting used to the squishy, stinking manure underneath him and looking around distastefully.

Just then another associate devil came into the room and announced, "All right, everyone, coffee break's over. Back on your heads."

———

Q: What's black and white and looks good with pinstripes?

A: A pit bull attacking a lawyer.

The farmer had sued the railroad for damages resulting from the death of one of his cows. After hours in court, the railway attorney was making every effort to rattle him.

"Tell me again," said the lawyer, "was the cow on the train line?"

"Well," said the weary farmer, "if you want to hear the truth, the cow was bathing in a brook on the opposite side of the bank when the engine saw it, leaped off the rails and over the fence, dashed down the bank, landed on the cow, and strangled it to death without a word."

Proud mother: "My son is a brilliant lawyer. He can look at a contract and tell you immediately whether it's oral or written."

Relaxing at home, attorney Kathy Feinblatt was approached by a group of Jehovah's Witnesses. She told them she hadn't seen the accident, but that she'd be interested in taking the case.

For certain people, after fifty, litigation takes the place of sex.
—Gore Vidal

Dolin was being badgered by attorney Susan George in a thorough and painful cross-examination.

"You're sure, sir, that it was exactly five minutes?"

"Yes, ma'am, I am. I said it before. Five minutes."

"I'm going to give you a test," the lawyer persisted.

The jury waited expectantly as she removed a stopwatch from her briefcase and said, "Tell me when exactly five minutes have elapsed."

At the end of exactly five minutes, Dolin shouted, "Time's up."

After losing the case, Ms. George was very curious. She walked over to the witness and asked, "Tell me, Mr. Dolin, how is it that you can tell time so exactly?"

"Easy," replied Dolin, "by the clock on the wall behind you."

Turnbull, a wealthy New York City attorney, decided to take a few days' vacation and visit his poor cousin out in the countryside.

Relaxing on the porch swing with his relative, he glanced at the surroundings and said, "Henry, you ought to have studied the law. Why, not a man alive could enjoy living in this squalor. I make a thousand bucks a day, easy."

The country cousin was astonished. "Honest?"

"What's the difference?"

A meek little man was hauled into court and stood shamefully before the judge, who asked him to explain the situation.

"I was arrested for resisting an officer."

"Resisting an officer!" said the justice in disbelief.

"Yes. He wanted fifty, I offered him forty."

"That one's not for sale. It's my ex-wife's lawyer."

Charlotte was astounded to see that her attorney's bill was $2,300. She demanded that he send her an itemized bill, which he did:

Consultation: $300

Court appearance: $500

Waking up at night and thinking about your case: $1,500

"How long have you known the defendant, Mr. O'Reilly?"

"Ten years, sir."

"Please tell the court, Mr. O'Reilly, whether you think he is the sort of man who would steal this money."

"How much was it again?"

The judge peered down at the disheveled man. "I must charge you for murder."

"All right," the man answered brightly, "what do I owe you?"

"Do you claim this man hit you with malice aforethought?" asked the lawyer.

"Look, smartass, you can't mix me up that easy," replied the elderly man. "I said he hit me with a Ford, and I'm sticking to it."

A law firm is successful when it has more clients than partners.
—Henny Youngman

Judge Landau glared with open hostility at the delinquent before him.

"You no-good druggie, have you ever earned an honest dollar?" he hissed.

"Sure have, Your Honor," he answered brazenly, "when I voted for you last election."

Lucy joyfully placed a long-distance call from New York to her mother in Wyoming.

"Great news, Mother! Irving passed the bar exam, and we're going to get married next week!"

"Well, sweetie, you tell him how proud and happy I am," said Lucy's mother. "But don't you think you ought to wait till he's been practicing for a year or two?"

"But, Mother," said Lucy, "we've been practicing!"

The judge faced the man before him and said, "Now, Lieutenant Peartree, according to records subpoenaed from the police department, you are not and never have been a member of the police force. Can you tell me how you came to claim your title?"

The plaintiff looked up. "It's kind of like the 'Honorable' in front of your name, sir. It don't mean a thing."

Knock knock.
Who's there?
Attorney Almi.
Attorney Almi who?
Attorney all my money over to the guy and he lost the damned case.

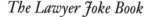

The priest was instructing a class of third-graders at All Saints grammar school.

"There were two brothers, and one of them chose the wicked path of Satan. The brother was evil and corrupt and did great damage to many people, and wound up a convicted criminal in a tiny, dark cell.

"But the other brother studied hard and became a great, rich, knowledgeable lawyer.

"Now, children, what is the difference between these two brothers, who started out in the same place, who together embarked upon life's stormy seas?"

Herman raised his hand and said, "Easy. One of them got caught."

It was so cold one day last February that I saw a lawyer with his hands in his own pockets.
—Robert Peterson

Morgan was having great difficulty putting together a defense for his case.

"Ladies and gentlemen, this boy grew up in a . . . no, no, no . . . Albert had been trying to express his anger to his teacher, but she would often — no, no, that's no good. Albert is not a juvenile delinquent—he is merely an active, precocious little boy with homicidal tendencies . . ."

Deems FitzHugh, notorious airhead and son of wealthy New York attorney FitzHugh Senior, went to NYU Law School. His father promised him $10,000 if he made Law Review in his second year. One night the young FitzHugh called his father in excitement.

"Dad, Dad, guess what! Great news, Dad, you're gonna be thrilled!"

"Yes, son, what is it? What? Tell me!"

"I'm saving you $10,000!"

Lawsuit: *n.* a machine which you go into as a pig and come out of as a sausage
—Ambrose Bierce

Liz opened her first law textbook and scanned the table of contents:

pages 1-3 .... Libel Law
pages 4-8 .... Divorce Law
pages 9-12 .... Criminal Law
pages 13-627 .... Loopholes

The prosecuting attorney faced the witness.

"Isn't it true the defendant talks to himself when alone?"

"Couldn't say. Never been with him when he was alone."

The lecture room had erupted into a loud, angry argument and the law professor attempted to restore order. He cried out, "Order! Order!"

A student shouted back, "Beer!"

John Kelly, a divorce lawyer, met a colleague of his in a bar after a long day.

"I had a ninety-five-year-old couple in the office today asking for a divorce. I asked them why they waited so long. They told me they were waiting till the children were dead."

———

Cara Prewitt was pleading her first case. She had been retained by a farmer to prosecute a railway company for running over twenty-four hogs.

She wanted to impress the jury with the magnitude of the injury and said, "Twenty-four hogs, ladies and gentlemen! Twenty-four! Twice the number there are in the jury box."

———

Identifying criminals is up to each of us. Usually they can be recognized by their large cuff links and their failure to stop eating when the man next to them is hit by a falling anvil.
—Woody Allen

———

Josephine Choffee, a young lawyer with a large firm, spent most of her time trying to give the appearance of being a successful and prosperous attorney; one day, upon leaving her office for lunch, she left a note on her door reading, "Will be back in an hour."

Upon her return she found that a rival from down the hall had inscribed on the sign, "What for?"

The defense lawyer began his summation. "Ladies and gentlemen of the jury, the plaintiff called my client, Mr. O'Keefe, an Irish scoundrel, as the evidence has shown."

The lawyer then pointed to the prosecuting attorney. "Now, Mr. Brown, I ask you, if he had called you an African-American scoundrel, what would you have done?

"Or you, Mr. Applebaum," he said, pointing to the judge, "if he had called you a Jewish scoundrel?"

He turned back to the jury. "Or any of you ladies and gentlemen—what would you have done if he had called you the kind of scoundrels you all are?"

Young attorney Pellichero had been discoursing for nearly seven hours to a weary jury, and finally he completed his summation

His opponent, a grizzled old veteran, arose and looked sweetly at the judge.

"Your Honor, I will follow the example of my young friend here who has just finished, and submit the case without argument."

Lawyer: One skilled in circumvention of the law.
Liar: A lawyer with a roving commission.
—Ambrose Bierce

Kate Smith, a young lawyer, was trying her first case before Justice Blom. She had evidently memorized her entire argument and had proceeded

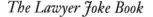

for ten minutes with her oratorical effort when the judge banged his gavel down and decided the case in her favor. Despite this, the young lawyer would not stop. It seemed as though she had attained such momentum that she could not be interrupted.

Finally, Justice Blom leaned forward and said, in his politest tone, "Counselor, notwithstanding your arguments, the court has decided this case in your favor."

———

A suburban widow was discussing her troubles with her best friend.

"Don't talk to me about lawyers," she said. "I've had so much trouble over John's property that sometimes I wish he hadn't died."

———

"What's a lawyer, Dad?" asked the young boy.

"A lawyer, son, is a man who induces two

other men to strip for a fight, and then runs off with their clothes."

Counselor Gaynor was interviewing prospective jurors before the trial.

"Do you know anything about this trial?" he asked one of them.

"Nope."

"Have you heard anything about it?"

"Nope."

"Have you read anything about it?"

"Can't read."

"Have you formed any opinion about this case?"

"What case?"

"Your Honor, the defense accepts this man."

Q. Why does California have all the lawyers and New Jersey have all the toxic waste dumps?

A. Because New Jersey had first choice!

"Do you suppose I'll have justice done to me?" the anxious criminal inquired of his attorney.

"I'm afraid you won't," replied the lawyer coldly. "I see two men on the jury who are opposed to hanging."

The tiresome jury selection process continued, each side hotly contesting and dismissing potential jurors. Don O'Brian was called for his question session.

"Property holder?"

"Yes, I am, Your Honor."
"Married or single?"
"Married for twenty years, Your Honor."
"Formed or expressed an opinion?"
"Not in twenty years, Your Honor."

If law school is so hard to get through, how come there are so many lawyers?
—Calvin Trillin

The trial was about to start; the defendant, jury, and lawyers were all assembled. Just then, one of the jury members raised her hand, and the judge motioned her to speak.

"I'm afraid I cannot serve as a juror, Your Honor. One look at that man convinces me he is guilty."

The judge sighed.

"That's the district attorney, Mrs. Atkinson."

The trial was just about to begin when the judge noticed that one of the jurors was missing.

"Where is Mr. Haley?" demanded the judge.

"Oh, that's my brother," replied the jury foreman, "but don't worry, Your Honor, he's left his verdict with me."

The young prisoner was on trial and had decided to represent himself rather than avail himself of the services of a public defender. Before proceeding with the case, the judge spoke to him solemnly.

"This is a very serious offense you're being charged with, young man. If you're convicted, it will mean a long term of imprisonment as well as a heavy fine. Have you no attorney to counsel you in your defense?"

The youngster did not seem at all perturbed; he looked around the courtroom and then approached the bench. With a confident grin,

he cheerfully replied, "Well, Your Honor, I don't have no lawyer, but I'm pleased to inform you that I have some real pals on the jury."

———

It takes a whole lot of suits to keep a lawyer well dressed.
  —Henny Youngman

———

"I can't keep the visitors in the reception area," the new receptionist said to the attorney in frustration. "I know you're working on an important case, but when I say you're out, they just don't believe me. They say they must see you."

The lawyer looked up from his paper-strewn desk.

"Well, just tell them 'That's what they all say,'" replied the busy man. "I don't care if you're insolent and obnoxious. I must prepare for

tomorrow's case, and I can't be disturbed anymore!"

Later that afternoon a woman presented herself at the front desk and insisted that she see the attorney. The receptionist assured her it was not possible, and flatly refused to let her by.

"But I'm his wife! I must see him," she protested.

"That's what they all say," replied the receptionist.

Two young public defenders, Liz and Norma, had exhausted themselves all afternoon hastily putting together a case to defend Julio, a psychiatric patient.

"I'm telling you, Liz, I'm starting to feel schizophrenic."

"That makes four of us."

Posted in the laboratory of a big cosmetics company was the following notice:

Due to the great increase of actions by the animal-rights groups against testing cosmetics on rats, our laboratory will immediately begin to use lawyers to test its products.

The reasons for this change are:

A. There is no shortage of lawyers.
B. Lab technicians won't get too attached to them.
C. There are things you simply can't get a rat to do.

A new restaurant, owned by two lawyers, one Japanese and the other Jewish, opened up last week in Orange County. It's called So-Sue-Me.

Overheard in a posh SoHo bar: "I got even with that lawyer who blackballed me at the club. His bitchy wife came to see me about divorcing him and I praised him so highly she decided not to do it."

Danny Kaputnik was an ambitious young attorney just establishing his practice in affluent Forest Hills. He was eager to make a name for himself and start reaping the rewards of a professional career; he visualized a life adorned by lavish parties, high-society women, and best of all, a glamorous, coveted reputation.

In planning for his imminent success and

prosperity, the young lawyer mortgaged his future to the hilt. He bought an expensive and beautiful home, hired an entire staff of servants, and bought expensive cars, clothing, and other trappings of success for himself and his beautiful young wife.

Unfortunately, his skill fell short of his aspirations, and he was unable to build a steady clientele; he lost several very public, prominent cases, and business grew steadily worse until he had lost all but a handful of the most routine and lackluster clients.

Finally, he realized that he was so deeply in debt he was in danger of bankruptcy. He sat down and thought, and reluctantly decided he and his wife would have to lower their standard of living.

He called his wife into the study and said, "Becky, I'm afraid we can't continue like this any longer; we're going to cut every imaginable corner, starting right now. We've both got to start making sacrifices. Now, if you'd only learn how to clean decently, we could fire the maid."

Without missing a beat, his wife replied, "Sweetie, if you'd only learn how to screw decently, we could fire the gardener."

"Thirty years. Want to sell that tie?"

I learned law so well, the day I graduated I sued the college, won the case, and got my tuition back.
—Fred Allen

Did you hear about the new law firm of Dewey, Cheatam, and Howe?

It was the long-awaited day of the trial, and poor McWaters was jittery as a cat as the jury filed into the room and took their seats. He leaned nervously in toward his lawyer and whispered, "Hey! How come the other guy has two lawyers?"

The attorney patted his client on the shoulder. "Don't worry, it's a very common practice.

One of them does the thinking while the other one does the talking."

McWaters thought for a second, then said, "So who's doing your thinking?"

———

A lawyer's dream of heaven—every man reclaimed his property at the resurrection, and each tried to recover it from all his forefathers.
—Samuel Butler

———

Lawsuit: what a lawyer wears to work.

A small news item in the *Daily Gazette* mentioned a legal breakthrough in Polish car insurance: it's called "My Fault."

It was Prohibition, and John Lanigan had been arrested and charged with selling liquor. But he had an unshakable defense; his attorney, in addressing the jury, asked the justice and the jury to look carefully at the defendant. They studied Mr. Lanigan closely, then returned their gaze to his distinguished counselor.

A dramatic pause ensued. Then the lawyer said, "Now, gentlemen of the jury, do you honestly think that if that man was to get his hands on a pint of whiskey, he'd sell it?"

Q. What do you have when there is one lawyer in town?

A. Too little work.

Q. What do you have when there are two lawyers in town?

A. Too much work.

Q. What do you need when you have three lawyers up to their necks in cement?

A. More cement.

The penalty for laughing in the courtroom is six months in jail: if it were not for this penalty, the jury would never hear the evidence.
—H. L. Mencken

Two old Jewish men are sitting on a park bench. One of them turns to the other and says, "Today is the proudest day of my life. Today my son graduated from law school."

The other looks at him and asks, "NYU?"

The first man shrugs, "And why not?"

Lawyer: One who protects us against robbers by taking away the temptation.
—H.L. Mencken

The two lawyers met on the street.

"So, Finkel, what happened to that case you were handling? The one where the son murdered his mother and father."

Finkel smiled. "Wonderful. I got him off with a light sentence."

The first lawyer was astonished. "But how?"

"Easy. I pleaded for mercy from the court because my client was an orphan!"

It was early evening at the trendy West Side bar and men and women, mostly young and wearing black, were standing at the bar eyeing the room. Two young women, one blonde and one brunette, watched as a rugged, good-looking man entered the bar, walked to the stool next to them, and ordered a drink.

"Hello there, big boy," the blonde purred. "I

haven't seen you before. What's your story?"

The man took a long pull on his drink. "I was married and living in New Jersey with a wife I couldn't stand. One night I finally had enough of her whining. So I took a gun and shot her a dozen times and dumped her body in the Hudson River. Then I called the best lawyer in three states, and he convinced a jury that it was justifiable homicide. All I got was six months in prison. And I just got out."

He leered up at the two. "So what do you think about that?"

The blonde leaned over to her friend and hissed, "He's single!"

A lawyer is never entirely comfortable with a friendly divorce, any more than a good mortician wants to finish the job and then have the patient sit up on the table.
—Jean Kerr

Mrs. Bates's late husband had been an estate lawyer. After many years, she was able to contact him through the help of a spiritual medium. "Oh, Lloyd," she cried, "it's been so awful without you! I don't know where to begin sorting my life out—the will, the estate is all in a mess—tell me, what should I do? where should I begin?"

Came a distant, ghostly voice, "You'll have to make an appointment with my secretary."

The courtroom was pregnant with anxious silence as the judge solemnly considered his verdict in the paternity suit before him. Suddenly, he reached into the folds of his robes, drew out a cigar, and ceremoniously handed it to the defendant.

"Congratulations. You have just become a father."

There was a young lawyer who showed up at a revival meeting and was asked to deliver a prayer. Unprepared, he gave a prayer straight from his lawyer's heart: "Stir up much strife amongst thy people, Lord," he prayed, "lest thy servant perish."

—Senator Sam Ervin

After the trial had been going on for three days, Finley, the man accused of committing the crimes, stood up and approached the judge's bench.

"Your Honor, I would like to change my plea from innocent to guilty of the charges."

The judge angrily banged his fist on the desk. "If you're guilty, why didn't you say so in the first place and save this court a lot of time and inconvenience?" he demanded.

Finley looked up wide-eyed. "Well, when the trial started I thought I was innocent, but that was before I heard all the evidence against me."

Q: The tooth fairy, a high-priced lawyer, and a low-priced lawyer were in a room. There was a $100 bill lying on a nearby table. Then the lights suddenly went out. When the lights came back on, the bill was gone. Who took it?

A: The high-priced lawyer took it, because the other two are only figments of your imagination.

A judge is a law student who marks his own examination papers.
—H. L. Mencken

A HASTY SETTLEMENT
by Ambrose Bierce, 1899

"Your Honor," said an Attorney, rising, "what is the present status of this case—as far as it has gone?"

"I have given a judgement for the residuary legatee under the will," said the Court, "put the costs upon the contestant, decided all questions relating to fees and other charges; and in short, the estate in litigation has been settled, with all controversies, disputes, misunderstandings and differences of opinion thereunto appertaining."

"Ah, yes, I see," said the Attorney, thoughtfully. "We are making progress—we are getting on famously."

"Progress?" echoed the Judge—"progress? Why, sir, the matter is concluded!"

"Exactly, exactly; it had to be concluded in order to give relevancy to the motion that I am about to make. Your Honor, I move that the judgement of the Court be set aside and the case reopened."

"Upon what grounds, sir?" the Judge asked in surprise.

"Upon the ground," said the Attorney, "that

after paying all the fees and expenses of litigation and all the charges against the estate there will be something left."

"There may have been an error," said his Honor, thoughtfully—"the Court may have underestimated the value of the estate. The motion is taken under advisement."

———

Doctors and lawyers must go to school for years and years, often with little sleep and with great sacrifice to their first wives.

—Roy Blount, Jr.

———

Supreme Court: The place where the finest legal minds in the country gather—to serve as law clerks to the justices.

—Daniel R. White

"I still think we could've gotten a better deal had we plea bargained."

A judge is a man who ends a sentence with a sentence.
—Henny Youngman

A man and his wife were out on Sunday with their motorcycle group and were arrested for speeding. When they were brought before the judge the two of them started right in.

"In the first place, Your Honor," said the husband, "we weren't doing 50; it was much less than that. Maybe 35."

"Thirty-five!" the wife exclaimed. "We weren't doing anything near that. It couldn't have been more than 20 miles an hour."

One of the other club members jumped up. "Your Honor," he said, "I was following them, and believe me, they were almost at a standstill when the officer pulled them over."

The judge held his hands up. "Stop this right now before you folks back into something!"

———

Despite the best effort of lawyer Newman, the defendant was convicted of murder and sentenced to the electric chair. On the night before the execution he called Newman for any final words of advice.

The lawyer promptly replied, "Don't sit down."

———

The door to attorney Cooper's office opened slowly, and a bandaged and bruised middle-aged man painfully dragged himself in and sat down.

"You look like you need a doctor more than a lawyer," said Cooper. "What can I do for you?"

Slowly he began. "I came home very late last night with beer on my breath and lipstick on my collar. For no reason at all my wife began

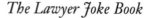

beating me with a baseball bat. Then she got tired and called her two brothers who live down the street, and they came over and kept hitting me with the bat."

He rubbed his head. "Is it legal for her to do that?"

Cooper spread his hands. "It's perfectly legal for a wife to hit her husband with a baseball bat—but she is not allowed to bring in any pinch hitters!"

The truly successful lawyer owns his own ambulance.
    —Henny Youngman

Bob Winegarten opened the morning paper and, after reading the front page, the sports, and the financial section, flipped to the obituaries. There was his name. Outraged, he rushed to the phone and called his lawyer.

"Sid, Sid," Winegarten cried, "This is Winegarten. Did you see the paper?"

His lawyer answered, "I did."

"Did you see my name in the obits? I want to sue!"

There was a long pause. "Winegarten, where are you calling from?"

An incompetent attorney can delay a trial for months or years. A competent attorney can delay one even longer.
—Evelle J. Younger

O'Sullivan, Cabot, Kelly and Mendlebaum was one of the most successful law firms in New York. Of all the partners, Mendlebaum brought in the most business. Lunching with him one day, a curious friend asked, "Why is your name listed last? O'Sullivan spends most of his time in the south of France, Cabot is at his club's bar every afternoon, and Kelly is at the race track all the time. Since you bring in all the business, your name should be first."

Mendlebaum beamed. "All my clients read from right to left."